LADYBIRD PICTURE DICTIONARY

Contents

Published by Ladybird Books Ltd
80 Strand London WC2R 0RL
A Penguin Company

19 17 15 14 16 18 20

© LADYBIRD BOOKS LTD MCMXCVI This edition MCMXCIX

LADYBIRD and the device of a Ladybird are trademarks of Ladybird Books Ltd

Picture Dictionary

compiled by GERALDINE TAYLOR
illustrated by GAYNOR BERRY

Aa

aeroplane

flying an aeroplane

animal

pet animals

acrobat

a circus acrobat

alligator

a green alligator

answer

6+4=10

the answer is ten

actor

an actor on the stage

alphabet

ABCDEFG
HIJKLMN
OPQRSTU
VWXYZ

letters of the alphabet

ant

a line of ants

address

Mr C Gull
3 Beach Road
Sandycliff

writing the address

ambulance

a hospital ambulance

apple

a shiny apple

advertisement

ZOOM

a car advertisement

anchor

a ship's anchor

apron

a clean apron

aquarium

fish in an aquarium

arm

a broken arm

arrow

a bow and arrow

artist

an artist painting

asleep

asleep in bed

astronaut

an astronaut on the moon

astronomer

an astronomer
looking at stars

atlas

THE
LADYBIRD
PICTURE
ATLAS

a world atlas

audience

a theatre audience

Bb

baby

a baby playing

bag

a shopping bag

baker

a baker making bread

ball

a beach ball

balloon

hot-air balloons

3

banana a ripe banana	**bee** bees around their nest	**blanket** wrapped in a blanket
basket a basket of washing	**bell** ringing a bell	**boat** a blue boat
bath having a bath	**bicycle** riding a bicycle	**bonfire** a big bonfire
bear a polar bear	**bird** a bird with a worm	**book** a funny book
bed bunk beds	**birthday** a birthday cake	**bottle** bottles of fizzy orange

box

a cat in a box

brush

a scrubbing brush

button

coloured buttons

boy

a boy fishing

bubble

blowing bubbles

Cc

breakfast

eating breakfast

bus

a bus stop

cactus

a prickly cactus

brick

building bricks

butcher

a butcher slicing meat

cake

chocolate cake

bridge

a bridge over the river

butterfly

a pretty butterfly

calculator

a pocket calculator

5

calendar

look at the calendar

castle

a castle and moat

chair

a rocking chair

camera

a camera and film

cat

a ginger cat

chimney

a chimney stack

canoe

paddling a canoe

caterpillar

a green furry caterpillar

chimpanzee

a baby chimpanzee

car

a racing car

cave

a dark cave

chocolate

a bar of chocolate

carpet

a roll of carpet

ceiling

a yellow ceiling

church

going to church

city

a big city

computer

a desk-top computer

Dd

clock

a wall clock

cook

a ship's cook

dancer

a ballet dancer

cloud

dark clouds

countryside

in the countryside

day

days of the week

clown

circus clowns

crowd

a crowd of people

dentist

at the dentist's

comb

a pink comb

cup

a cup of coffee

desert

a sandy desert

7

desk

an office desk

different

different shoes

dog

a sleepy dog

detective

a detective looking for clues

digger

a yellow digger

doll

a rag doll

diamond

a diamond ring

dinosaur

a spiky dinosaur

door

a brown door

dice

a pair of dice

diver

a deep-sea diver

dragon

a fiery dragon

dictionary

The Ladybird Picture Dictionary

a picture dictionary

doctor

a doctor on call

drawing

a drawing of a cat

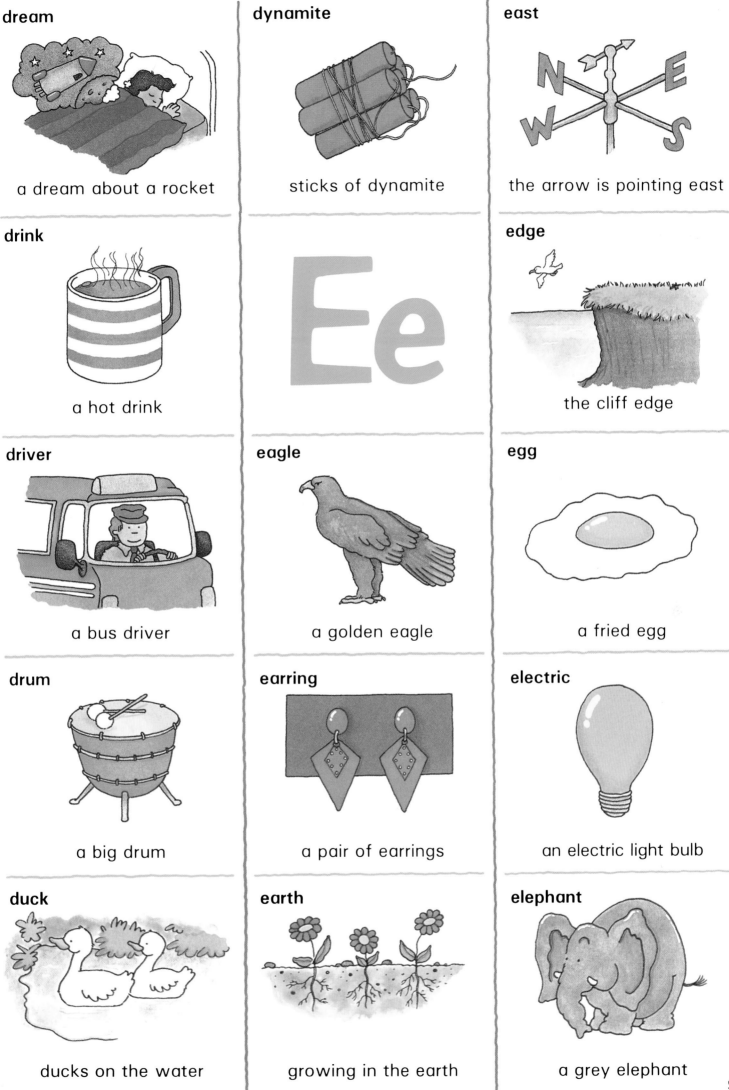

dream

a dream about a rocket

dynamite

sticks of dynamite

east

the arrow is pointing east

drink

a hot drink

Ee

edge

the cliff edge

driver

a bus driver

eagle

a golden eagle

egg

a fried egg

drum

a big drum

earring

a pair of earrings

electric

an electric light bulb

duck

ducks on the water

earth

growing in the earth

elephant

a grey elephant

engine

checking the engine

evening

the sun sets in the evening

explosion

a loud explosion

entrance

go in through the entrance

exhibition

an art exhibition

Ff

envelope

a brown envelope

exit

go out through the exit

farm

farm animals

equipment

diving equipment

experiment

a scientific experiment

feather

a peacock's feather

escalator

a moving escalator

explorer

an explorer on safari

fence

a wooden fence

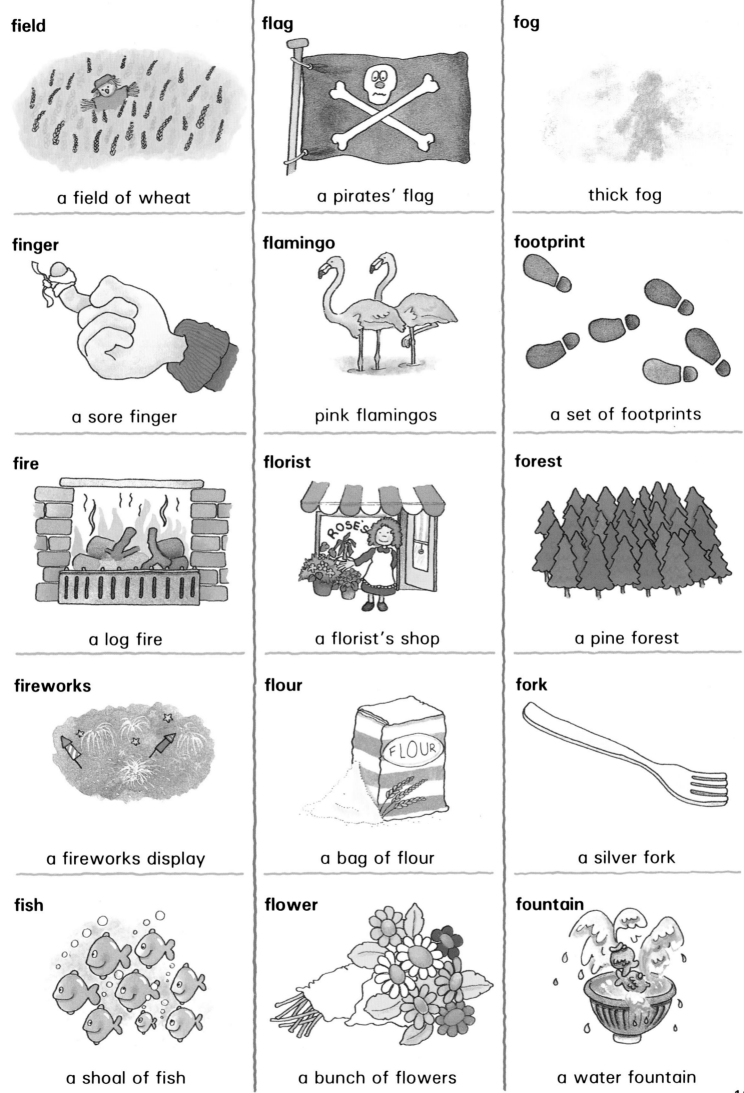

field

a field of wheat

flag

a pirates' flag

fog

thick fog

finger

a sore finger

flamingo

pink flamingos

footprint

a set of footprints

fire

a log fire

florist

a florist's shop

forest

a pine forest

fireworks

a fireworks display

flour

a bag of flour

fork

a silver fork

fish

a shoal of fish

flower

a bunch of flowers

fountain

a water fountain

11

friend

best friends

furniture

pieces of furniture

garden

digging the garden

frog

a jumping frog

Gg

gate

a wooden gate

frost

frost on the window

gale

trees blowing in a gale

ghost

a spooky ghost

fruit

a bowl of fruit

game

playing a game

giant

a happy giant

fur

a kitten with soft fur

garage

a double garage

girl

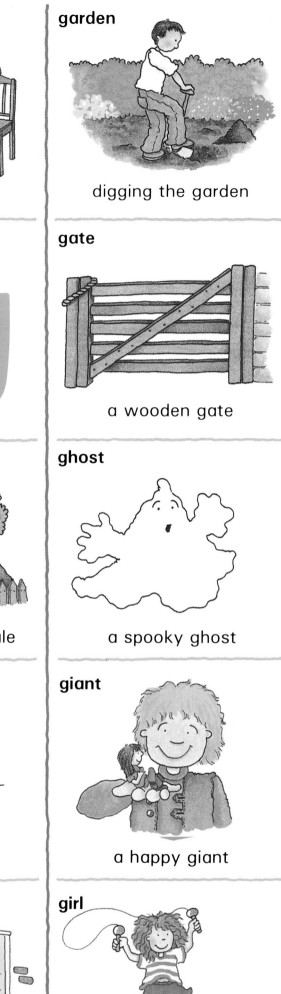

a girl skipping

12

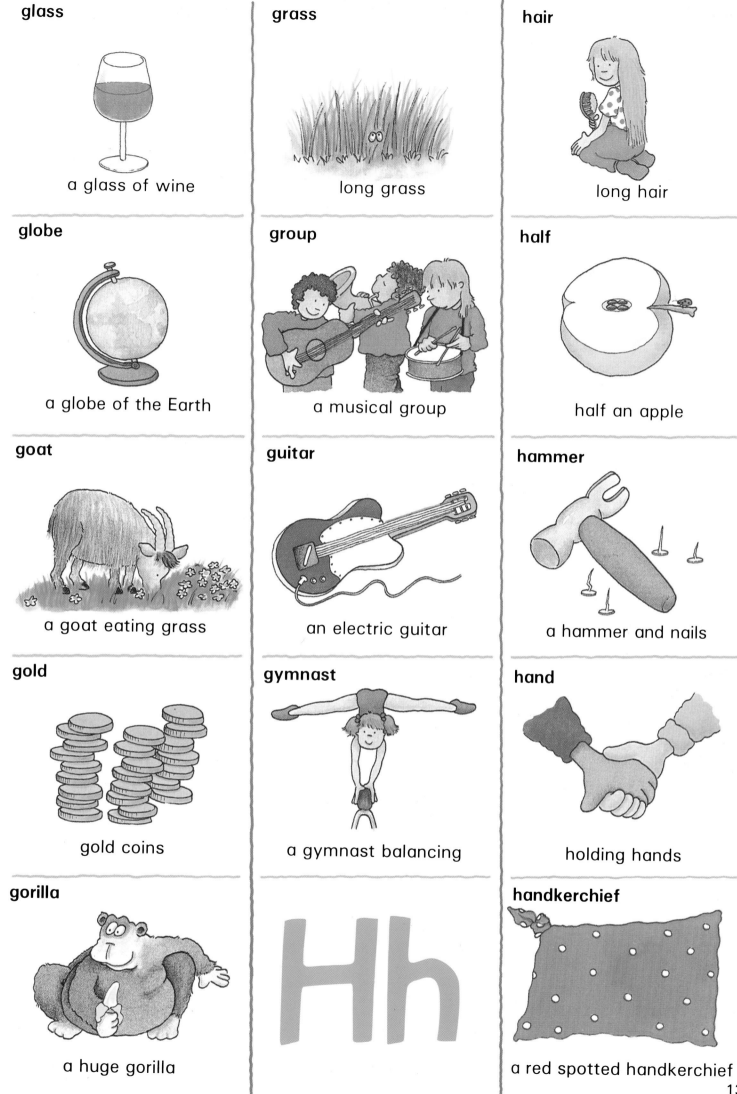

glass

a glass of wine

grass

long grass

hair

long hair

globe

a globe of the Earth

group

a musical group

half

half an apple

goat

a goat eating grass

guitar

an electric guitar

hammer

a hammer and nails

gold

gold coins

gymnast

a gymnast balancing

hand

holding hands

gorilla

a huge gorilla

Hh

handkerchief

a red spotted handkerchief

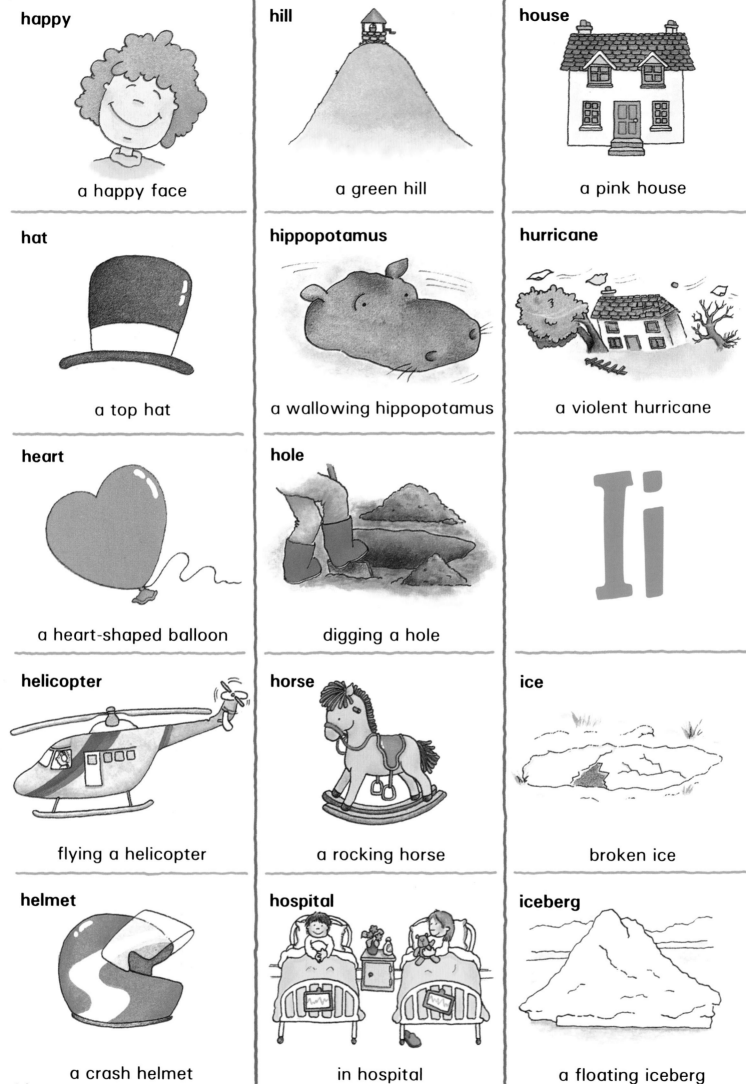

happy

a happy face

hill

a green hill

house

a pink house

hat

a top hat

hippopotamus

a wallowing hippopotamus

hurricane

a violent hurricane

heart

a heart-shaped balloon

hole

digging a hole

Ii

helicopter

flying a helicopter

horse

a rocking horse

ice

broken ice

helmet

a crash helmet

hospital

in hospital

iceberg

a floating iceberg

ice cream

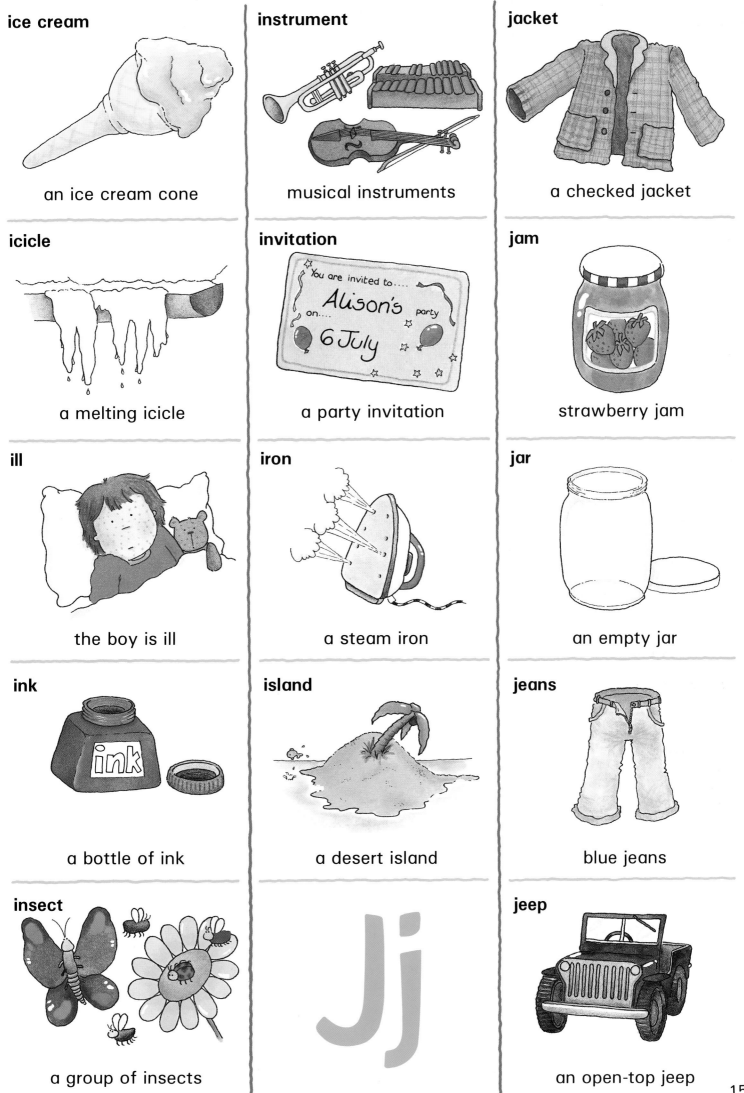

an ice cream cone

instrument

musical instruments

jacket

a checked jacket

icicle

a melting icicle

invitation

You are invited to....
Alison's party
on....
6 July

a party invitation

jam

strawberry jam

ill

the boy is ill

iron

a steam iron

jar

an empty jar

ink

ink

a bottle of ink

island

a desert island

jeans

blue jeans

insect

a group of insects

Jj

jeep

an open-top jeep

15

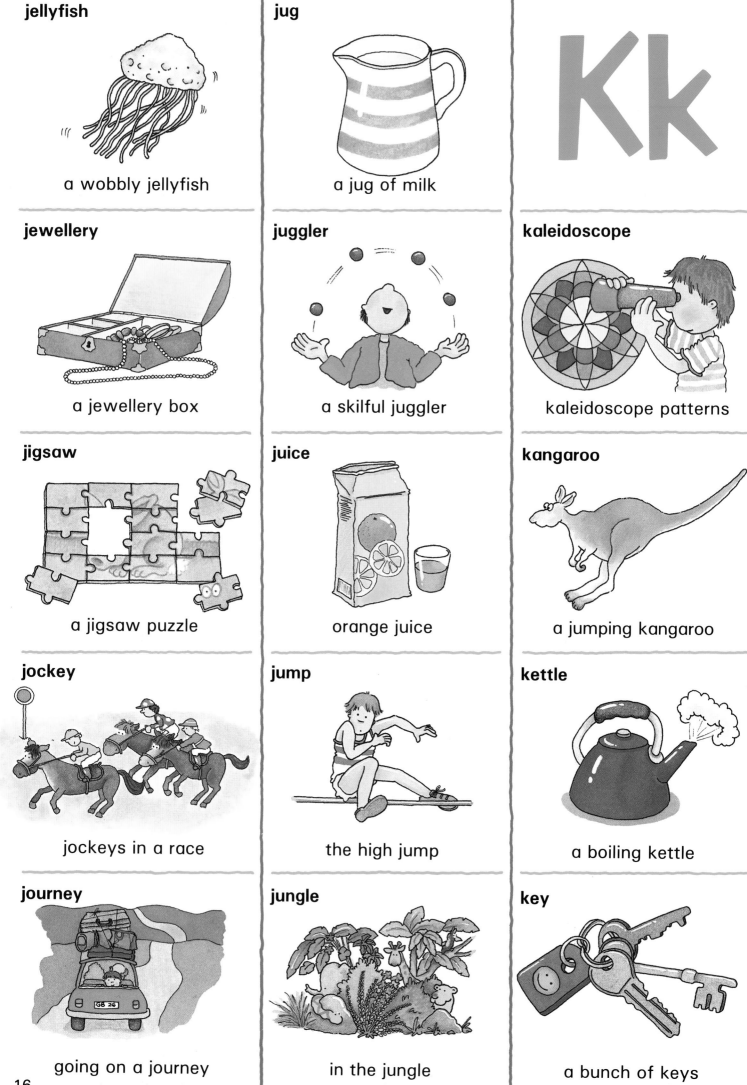

jellyfish

a wobbly jellyfish

jug

a jug of milk

Kk

jewellery

a jewellery box

juggler

a skilful juggler

kaleidoscope

kaleidoscope patterns

jigsaw

a jigsaw puzzle

juice

orange juice

kangaroo

a jumping kangaroo

jockey

jockeys in a race

jump

the high jump

kettle

a boiling kettle

journey

going on a journey

jungle

in the jungle

key

a bunch of keys

king  a king on his throne	**knife** cutting with a knife	**koala** a koala and its baby
kiss a kiss on the cheek	**knight** a knight in armour	**Ll**
kitchen cooking in the kitchen	**knitting** knitting a jumper	**label** a white label
kite flying a kite	**knob** a red door knob	**lace** a lace tablecloth
kitten a playful kitten	**knot** tying a knot	**ladder** a long ladder

17

ladybird

a red ladybird

lemon

a sliced lemon

lion

a roaring lion

lake

a boating lake

letter

writing a letter

loaf

loaves of bread

lamp

a table lamp

library

reading in the library

log

a log cabin

lawn

mowing the lawn

lid

a striped tin lid

luggage

a lot of luggage

leaf

a green leaf

lightning

thunder and lightning

Mm

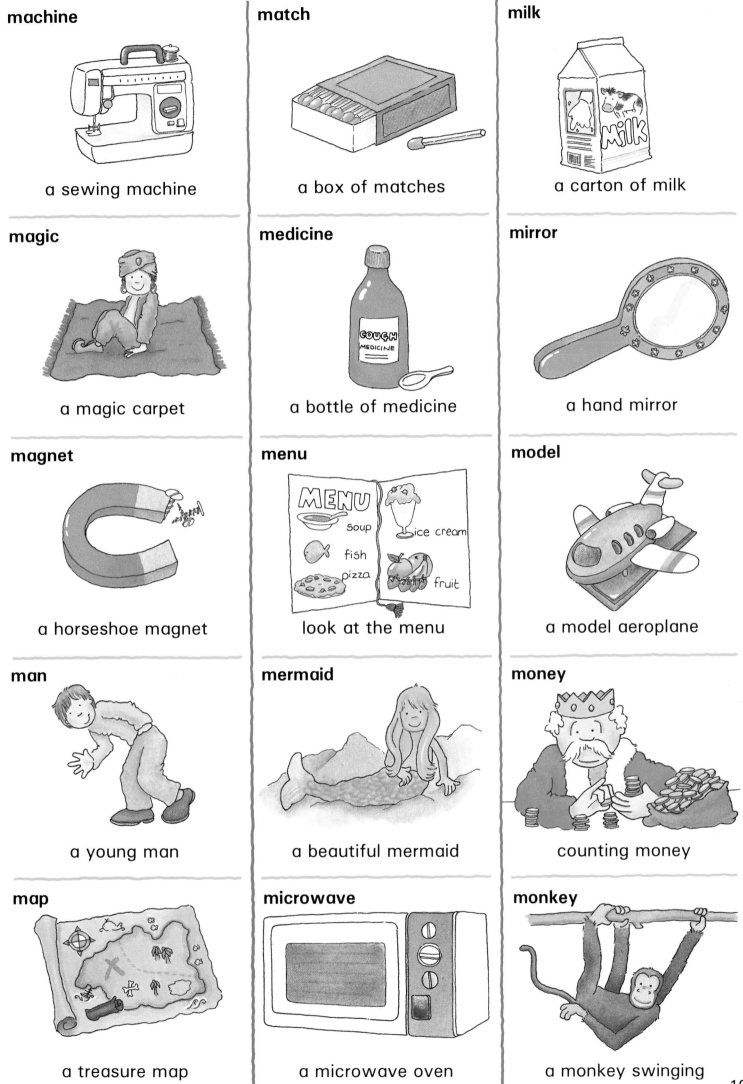

machine

a sewing machine

match

a box of matches

milk

a carton of milk

magic

a magic carpet

medicine

a bottle of medicine

mirror

a hand mirror

magnet

a horseshoe magnet

menu

look at the menu

model

a model aeroplane

man

a young man

mermaid

a beautiful mermaid

money

counting money

map

a treasure map

microwave

a microwave oven

monkey

a monkey swinging

19

moon

a crescent moon

mud

covered in mud

nature

Class 3b

a nature display

morning

the sun rises in the morning

museum

visiting a museum

necklace

a ruby necklace

motorcycle

riding a motorcycle

Nn

needle

a needle and thread

mountain

snow-capped mountains

nail

a box of nails

neighbour

next-door neighbours

mouse

a mouse nibbling cheese

name

Megan   Billy
Jenny
Robert   Peter

name tags

nest

a bird's nest

net

a fishing net

north

the arrow is pointing north

oak

an oak tree

newspaper

reading the newspaper

notebook

a blue notebook

oar

wooden oars

night

a starry night

nurse

a hospital nurse

octopus

an octopus on a rock

nightmare

a scary nightmare

nut

a bag of nuts

office

a busy office

noise

a loud noise

Oo

oil

cans of oil

optician

at the optician's

outside

looking outside

palace

a grand palace

orange

peeling an orange

oven

a pie in the oven

panda

a black and white panda

orchard

an apple orchard

owl

a barn owl

paper

wrapping paper

ostrich

an ostrich running

Pp

parachute

a parachute jump

outline

drawing the outline

paint

a paint box

parrot

a colourful parrot

party

a birthday party

people

a group of people

piece

a piece of pie

path

a path across the field

photograph

a photograph album

pillow

a feather pillow

pea

peas in a pod

piano

a grand piano

pilot

an aeroplane pilot

pencil

coloured pencils

picnic

a picnic basket

planet

the planet Earth

penguin

a black and white penguin

picture

a picture of a boat

pocket

two big pockets

post office

at the post office

Qq

quilt

a patchwork quilt

prize

first prize

quarter

cut into quarters

quiz

a quiz show

puddle

splashing in a puddle

queen

a queen on her throne

Rr

puppet

a glove puppet

question

asking a question

what's your name?

rabbit

a pet rabbit

puppy

a hungry puppy

quiet

ssh...be quiet!

race

a running race

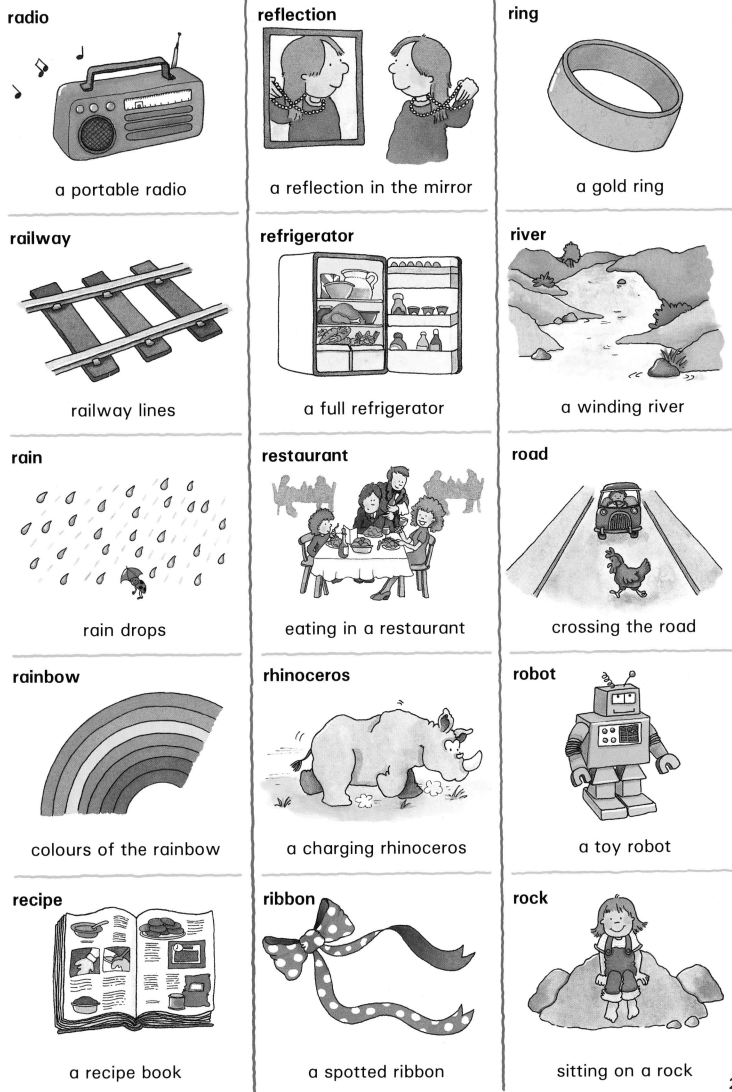

radio

a portable radio

reflection

a reflection in the mirror

ring

a gold ring

railway

railway lines

refrigerator

a full refrigerator

river

a winding river

rain

rain drops

restaurant

eating in a restaurant

road

crossing the road

rainbow

colours of the rainbow

rhinoceros

a charging rhinoceros

robot

a toy robot

recipe

a recipe book

ribbon

a spotted ribbon

rock

sitting on a rock

25

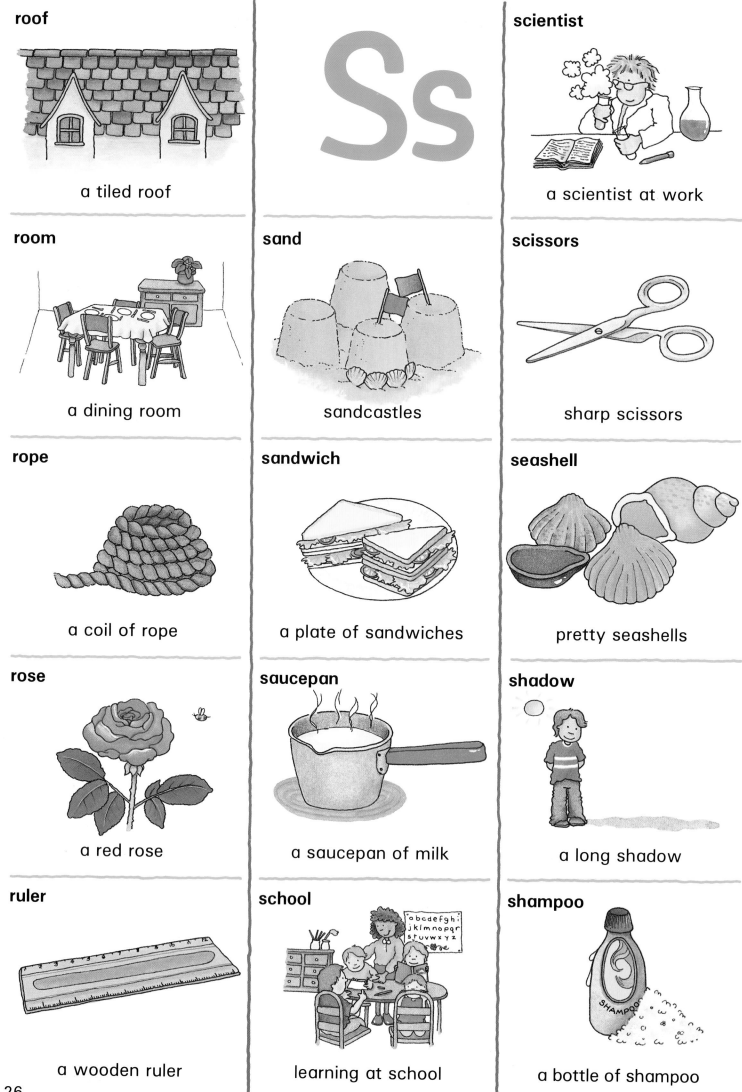

roof

a tiled roof

Ss

scientist

a scientist at work

room

a dining room

sand

sandcastles

scissors

sharp scissors

rope

a coil of rope

sandwich

a plate of sandwiches

seashell

pretty seashells

rose

a red rose

saucepan

a saucepan of milk

shadow

a long shadow

ruler

a wooden ruler

school

learning at school

shampoo

a bottle of shampoo

26

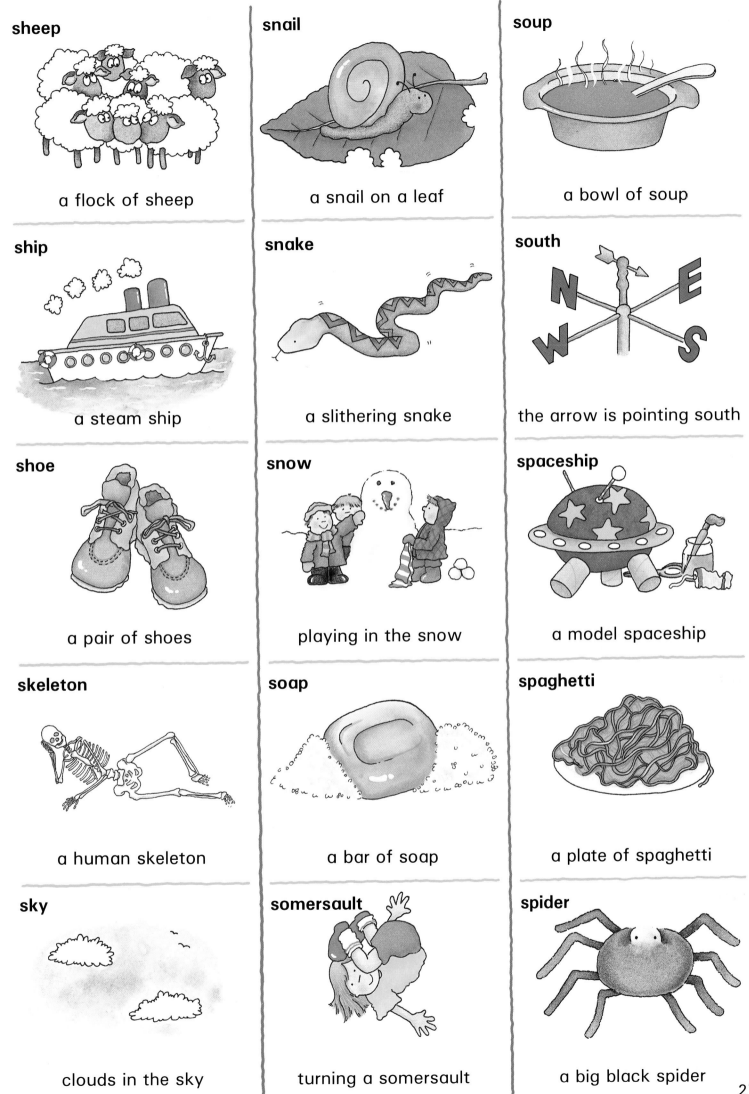

sheep

a flock of sheep

snail

a snail on a leaf

soup

a bowl of soup

ship

a steam ship

snake

a slithering snake

south

the arrow is pointing south

shoe

a pair of shoes

snow

playing in the snow

spaceship

a model spaceship

skeleton

a human skeleton

soap

a bar of soap

spaghetti

a plate of spaghetti

sky

clouds in the sky

somersault

turning a somersault

spider

a big black spider

27

square

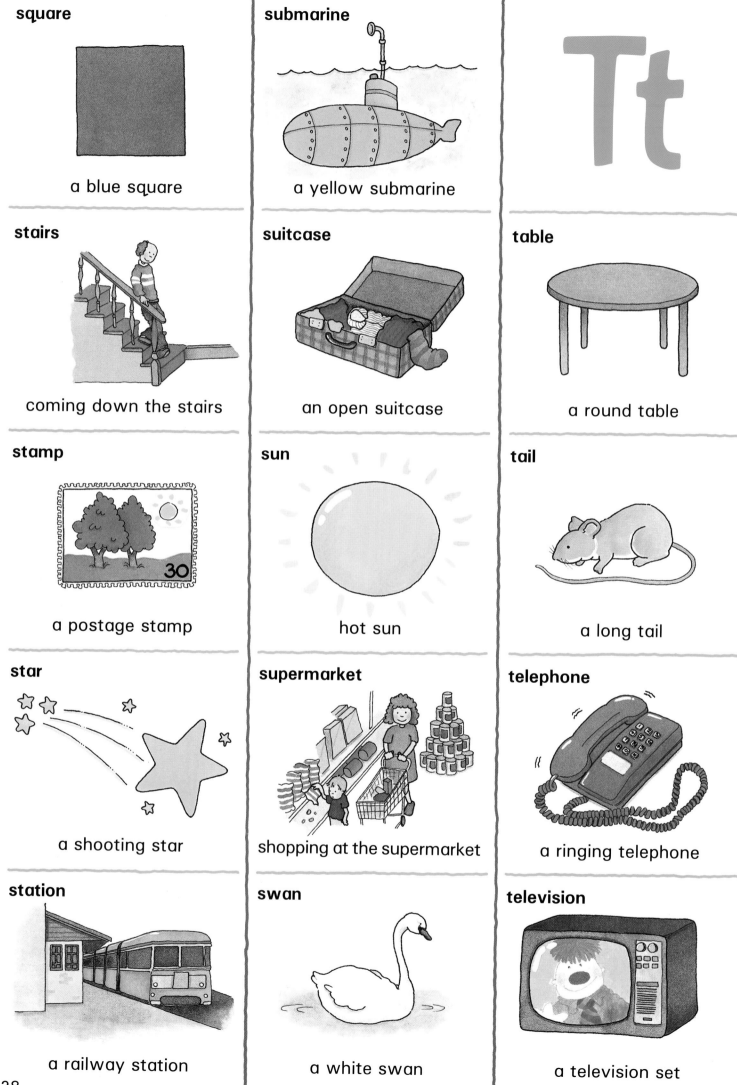

a blue square

submarine

a yellow submarine

Tt

stairs

coming down the stairs

suitcase

an open suitcase

table

a round table

stamp

a postage stamp

sun

hot sun

tail

a long tail

star

a shooting star

supermarket

shopping at the supermarket

telephone

a ringing telephone

station

a railway station

swan

a white swan

television

a television set

tent

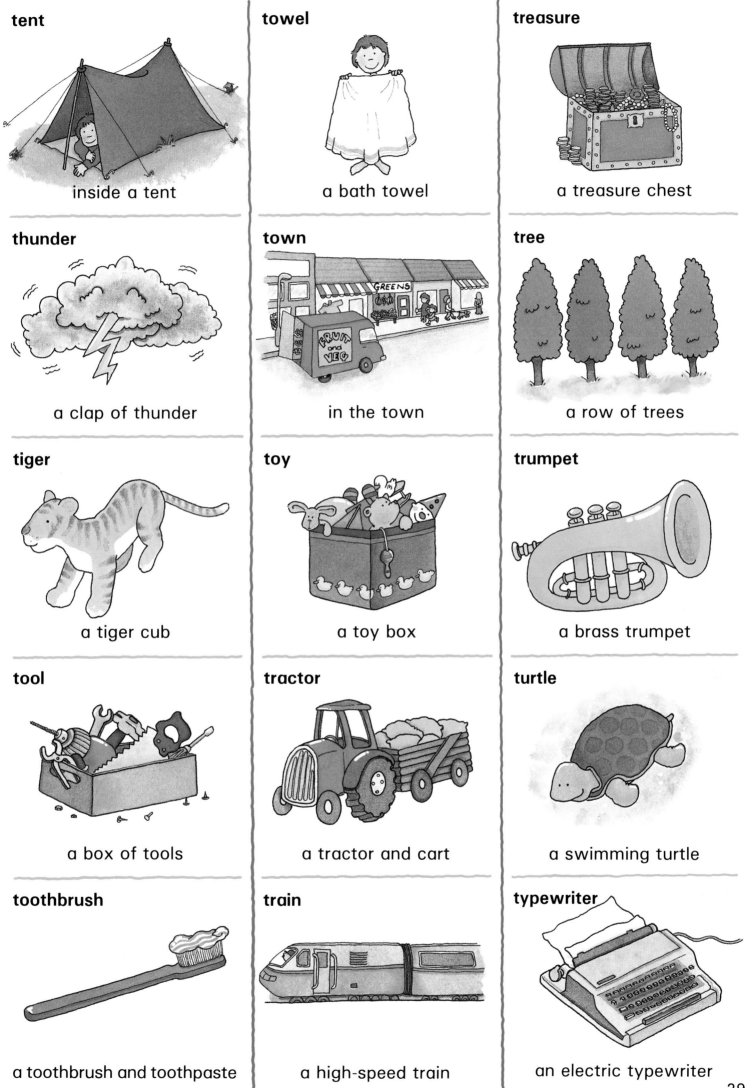

inside a tent

towel

a bath towel

treasure

a treasure chest

thunder

a clap of thunder

town

in the town

tree

a row of trees

tiger

a tiger cub

toy

a toy box

trumpet

a brass trumpet

tool

a box of tools

tractor

a tractor and cart

turtle

a swimming turtle

toothbrush

a toothbrush and toothpaste

train

a high-speed train

typewriter

an electric typewriter

29

Uu

uniform

a nurse's uniform

vase

a vase of flowers

ugly

an ugly mask

upside down

hanging upside down

vegetable

a box of vegetables

umbrella

an open umbrella

Vv

video

a video recorder

underground

a mole underground

vacuum cleaner

a powerful vacuum cleaner

view

a view of the sea

unicorn

a white unicorn

valley

a deep valley

village

a small village

violin

a violin and bow

wall

a brick wall

water

a jug of water

voice

a loud voice

wallet

a leather wallet

waterfall

a high waterfall

volcano

an erupting volcano

wallpaper

hanging wallpaper

wave

jumping over waves

Ww

wasp

a swarm of wasps

weather

a weather chart

walk

going for a walk

watch

a watch to tell the time

web

a spider's web

31

welcome

a warm welcome

whisker

six long whiskers

window

a broken window

west

the arrow is pointing west

whisper

a soft whisper

wolf

a grey wolf

whale

a blue whale

whistle

a silver whistle

woman

a woman reading

wheel

bicycle wheels

wind

blown off by the wind

world

a map of the world

wheelbarrow

a garden wheelbarrow

windmill

an old windmill

worm

a wriggly worm

Xx

X-ray

an X-ray photograph

xylophone

a wooden xylophone

Yy

yak

a hairy yak

yawn

a sleepy yawn

year

months of the year

yogurt

a pot of yogurt

yolk

two yolks!

yo-yo

a red and yellow yo-yo

Zz

zebra

a striped zebra

zip

a zip fastener

zodiac

signs of the zodiac

zoo

animals in the zoo

33

My body

ear

eyebrow

mouth

chin

lip

neck

hair

nose

tongue

eye

teeth

cheek

Clothes

shorts

mittens

pyjamas

blouse

scarf

shirt

tie

trousers

dress

sweater/jumper

sandals

boots

slippers

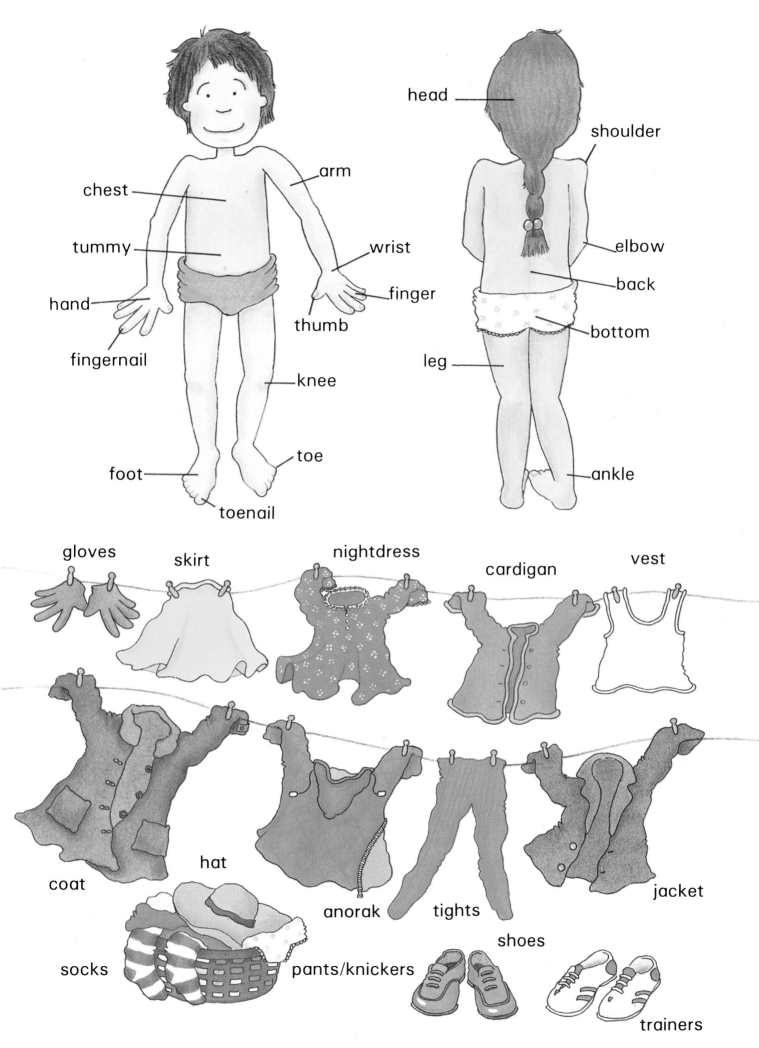

chest

arm

tummy

wrist

hand

finger

thumb

fingernail

knee

toe

foot

toenail

head

shoulder

elbow

back

bottom

leg

ankle

gloves

skirt

nightdress

cardigan

vest

coat

hat

anorak

tights

jacket

socks

pants/knickers

shoes

trainers

35

Families

grandad/grandpa

mother/mum

father/dad

son

granny/grandma

daughter

husband

sister

brother

wife

baby

uncle

cousin

aunt

twins

Food

biscuits

milk

chicken

jam

beefburger

ham

eggs

vegetables

juice

bread

salad

yogurt

sausages

sauce

cheese

meat

pizza

sugar

spaghetti

fruit

Shops

toy shop

butcher

greengrocer

florist

37

Numbers

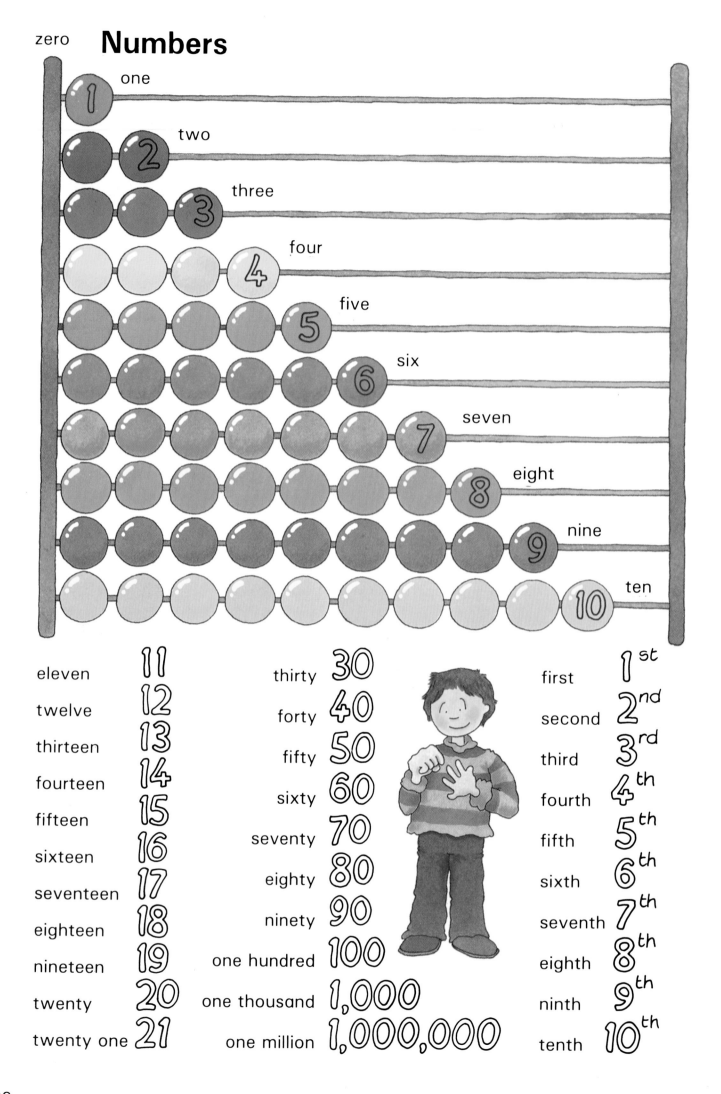

zero

one — 1
two — 2
three — 3
four — 4
five — 5
six — 6
seven — 7
eight — 8
nine — 9
ten — 10

eleven 11
twelve 12
thirteen 13
fourteen 14
fifteen 15
sixteen 16
seventeen 17
eighteen 18
nineteen 19
twenty 20
twenty one 21

thirty 30
forty 40
fifty 50
sixty 60
seventy 70
eighty 80
ninety 90
one hundred 100
one thousand 1,000
one million 1,000,000

first 1st
second 2nd
third 3rd
fourth 4th
fifth 5th
sixth 6th
seventh 7th
eighth 8th
ninth 9th
tenth 10th

Days of the week

Sunday	Thursday
Monday	Friday
Tuesday	Saturday
Wednesday	

Months of the year

January	July
February	August
March	September
April	October
May	November
June	December

Shapes and colours

a red rectangle

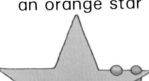

an orange star

a yellow heart

a green oval

a blue circle

a purple triangle

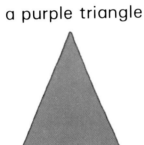

a pink square

a brown diamond

a black oval

a red heart

a grey rectangle

a white triangle

a turquoise diamond

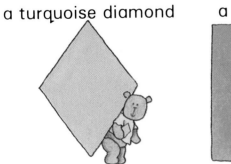

a green square

a yellow star

an orange circle

Doing words

read

sleep

sit

buy

dress

dry

sing

wash

write

pull

ride

push

wave

eat

jump

drink

walk

talk

run

stop

go

listen

40

Opposite words

hot

cold

tall

short

up

down

old

new

dirty

clean

empty

full

thin

fat

light

heavy

slow

on

off

fast

sad

happy

big

little

top

bottom

41

Words we write a lot

a	comes	had	made	play	up
about	coming	has	make	played	upon
after		have	me	playing	
all		having	more		
am	did	he	my		very
an	do	her	myself	said	
and	doing	here		saw	
are	down	him		see	want
as		his	new	she	was
at			nice	so	we
away	for		no	some	went
	from	I	not		were
		if			what
back		in		that	when
be	get	into	of	the	where
because	getting	is	off	their	who
but	go	it	old	them	with
	goes		on	then	
	going		only	there	
came	good	like	or	they	you
can	got	look	other	this	your
come		looking	our	to	

Spelling checklist

A

	Page		Page		Page		Page
a	42	arrow	3	bed	4	brown	39
about	42	artist	3	bee	4	brush	5
acrobat	2	as	42	beefburger	37	bubble	5
actor	2	asleep	3	bell	4	bus	5
address	2	astronaut	3	bicycle	4	but	42
advertisement	2	astronomer	3	big	41	butcher	5
aeroplane	2	at	42	bird	4	butcher's	37
after	42	atlas	3	birthday	4	butterfly	5
all	42	audience	3	biscuits	37	button	5
alligator	2	August	39	black	39	to buy	40
alphabet	2	aunt	36	blanket	4		
am	42	away	42	blouse	34		
ambulance	2			blue	39	**C**	
an	42	**B**		boat	4	cactus	5
anchor	2			body	34-35	cake	5
and	42	baby	3, 36	bonfire	4	calculator	5
animal	2	back	35, 42	book	4	calendar	6
ankle	35	bag	3	boots	34	came	42
anorak	35	baker	3	bottle	4	camera	6
answer	2	ball	3	bottom	35, 41	can	42
ant	2	balloon	3	box	5	canoe	6
apple	2	banana	4	boy	5	car	6
April	39	basket	4	bread	37	cardigan	35
apron	2	bath	4	breakfast	5	carpet	6
aquarium	3	be	42	brick	5	castle	6
are	42	bear	4	bridge	5	cat	6
arm	3, 35	because	42	brother	36	caterpillar	6